This book belongs to:

Billy Terry

From
Grandpa & Grandma
Roell
1990

This 1988 Muppet Press book is published by Longmeadow Press.
Distributed by The Crown Publishing Group,
225 Park Avenue South, New York, New York 10003
Printed in Italy

h g f e d c b a

Library of Congress Cataloging-in-Publication Data

Ross, Harry, 1951–
The Fraggles Alphabet Pie.

Summary: The Fraggles introduce the alphabet
as they have adventures with an apple pie.
[1. Puppets—Fiction   2. Pies—Fiction.
3. Alphabet]   I. Title.
PZ7.R719658Fr 1988   [E]   87-34857
ISBN 0-517-66488-7

The Fraggles Alphabet Pie

by Harry Ross   illustrated by Larry Di Fiori

Muppet Press

A picked an apple.

B baked it.

C carried it.

D drove past it.

E was excited by it.

F fought for it.

G got it.

H hollered for it.

I inspected it.

J jumped for it.

K

K kept it.

L lifted it.

M

M moved it.

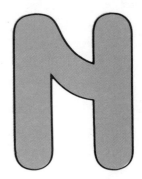

N nibbled at it.

O opened it.

P peeked at it.

Q quartered it.

R reached for it.

U upset it.

V vacuumed it.

W

W washed up after it.

X

X marked it.

Y yawned after eating it.

Z went to sleep and slept all night.